Town & County *Cameracolour Cameo*

Edinburgh

Photographs by *TREVOR WOOD*
Text by *JOHN MACKAY*

Town & County BOOKS

LONDON

A Member of the Ian Allan Group of Companies

First published 1984

ISBN 0 86364 012 5

Published by Town & County Books Ltd, Shepperton, Surrey;
and printed by Ian Allan Printing
at their works at Coombelands, Runnymede, England

INTRODUCTION

Edinburgh, veiled in a morning haze, revealed her skyline enchantingly in soft silhouette, at times vanishing, as a curtain of 'haar' (Scotch mist) lowered on to the roof tops of the Royal Mile.

Two girls, heavily rucksacked, stood on that thoroughfare of history looking lost.

'Can I help you?' I asked.

'We're looking for the Castle', said the one with the map.

On finding they had time to spare I suggested waiting for an hour or so by which time the haar would have lifted, and the Castle — and the views from its summit rock, would be seen in sunlight; meantime, would they allow me to direct them to old Parliament House?

Since we stood by St Giles' the High Kirk of Edinburgh, it was only a step or two to the Court of Session entrance in Parliament Square and so into the Great Hall of Parliament House.

The transformation brought an ejaculation of pleasure from both girls. From the greyness of outside in, to them, an ancient town still chilled and unfamiliar, they were confronted by a warm glow of amber light coming from high on the gilded hammerbeam roof, below which, advocates of the Scottish Law paced the polished floor, some alone, some in conversation, as they awaited the call to their case in one of the 12 courtrooms. These advocates, wigged and gowned in the style of the 18th century, made an animated picture bringing Old Edinburgh back to life for these young tourists.

Indeed, this one corner of the 'Old Town' is weighty with events in Scotland's story — and retains reminders of that past. Below the Great Hall, a banner carried at the battle of Flodden in 1513 still hangs. The hour bell of St Giles', although since recast, is the same bell that tolled the news of Scotland's defeat in that battle. And the old Tolbooth, originally a booth at which tolls were paid, has its outlines marked in brass on the causeway near the west-facing door of St Giles'.

By the time of Flodden, the Tolbooth had been enlarged to accommodate a prison and in 1532 the Court of Session used premises in the building as the meeting place for the College of Justice. Not until 1642 did the College move to what is now called Parliament House (begun in 1632, although the Scottish Parliament sat there only from 1639 until the Union of 1707).

As the year 1707 approached, so the Edinburgh folk who objected to the rumoured Union of the Scottish and English Parliaments demonstrated at the door of Parliament House; and in one other incident, overturned the Chancellor of Scotland's coach causing that much disturbed gentleman to flee with loss of all dignity down the narrow passage of the Close nearby.

Nevertheless, the Union came to pass and on that first day marking the marriage of the Parliaments, the music bells of St Giles' set out on the roof of the belfry were caused to play (by a ringer with a sense of humour?) a popular air of the time, beginning *How can I be sad on my wedding day.*

The Close by Parliament House was also the escape route for smuggler Robertson attending the service at St Giles' with his partner in crime, Wilson, before their execution. Both had been imprisoned in the adjacent Tolbooth and from there, an earlier bold attempt to win to freedom had failed.

The townsfolk hero-worshipped such daring, and at the execution of Wilson, they stoned the hangman. Captain Porteous of the Town Guard then ordered his men to fire on the mob who, in turn, subsequently accused Porteous of murder.

To placate the accusers, Porteous was imprisoned in the Tolbooth with every possibility that a pardon would be granted him when matters had calmed down — a situation not at all to the liking of the Edinburgh mob, 'one of the fiercest in Europe' who, with an unusual, an unnatural quietness, apart from the muffled beat of the borrowed Town drum, took Porteous from

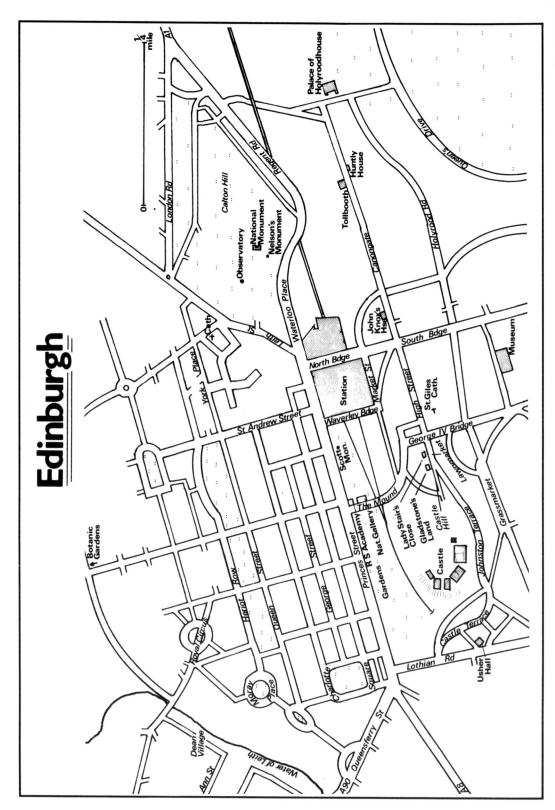

Edinburgh

Botanic Gardens

Dean Village

Ann St.

Water of Leith

A90 Queensferry St.

Royal Circus

Moray Place

Charlotte Square

Heriot Row

Queen Street

George Street

Princes Street

Lothian Rd

Usher Hall

Castle Terrace

Johnston Terrace

Grassmarket

Castle

Castle Hill

Gladstone's Land

Lady Stair's Close

Lawnmarket

George IV Bridge

St Giles Cath.

High Street

South Bdge

Museum

Market St

North Bdge

Station

Waverley Bdge

Scott Mon.

Gardens

Nat. Gallery

R.S. Academy

The Mound

St Andrew Street

York Place

Cath.

Leith St.

Waterloo Place

Regent Rd

Observatory

National Monument

Nelson's Monument

Calton Hill

London Rd

A1

¼ mile

0

Canongate

Tollbooth

John Knox's Hse.

Huntly House

Holyrood Rd

Queen's Drive

Palace of Holyroodhouse

the Tolbooth, marched him down by torchlight to Grassmarket and there, hanged him.

A young lawyer unwittingly witnessed this deed on his first night in Edinburgh and decided to leave such a town the next morning — but had second thoughts and stayed — to become Judge Lord Monboddo, a notable eccentric. See him leave the courts at Parliament House at the end of the working day. It is raining. Monboddo calls for a sedan chair. Places his *wig* therein, and stumps off alongside down the High Street to his lodging!

Lords, other than those of the Law — the Knights of the Most Noble Order of the Thistle, robe in the Signet Library adjoining Parliament Hall from where they walk in procession when called to attend a service in the Thistle Chapel of St Giles' when the Sovereign is in residence at the Palace of Holyroodhouse.

All such ceremonial was dear to Sir Walter Scott who once walked the Great Hall as a man of the Law. He called his master novel *The Heart of Midlothian* which was his nickname for the Tolbooth, its site now centred in the design of a heart by the west door of the Kirk.

One final scene in Parliament Square — one of modern times and at night: in the subdued lighting, strange shadows are cast on the now Georgian front of the Courts and Parliament House . . . the distant clatter of horses' hooves disturbs the quiet and into the empty Square, to circle the equestrian statue of Charles II before coming to a halt by the arcaded front, the kettle-drummer of the Royal Scots Greys on his black drum-horse enters, followed by the trumpeters of that regiment 'Second to None'. They had but recently played a fanfare to herald the opening of the Tattoo on the esplanade of the Castle of Edinburgh and now await their return for the Grand Finale. Here again, the picturesque past had come to life as has already been demonstrated in this introduction — played on a 'stage' occupying little more than a few yards at this heart of the Old Town.

Time now, to move on and explore.

We might follow the drummer and trumpeters back to the Castle for a starting point, at the Tattoo; or better still, go in

Canongate Tolbooth.

imagination behind the scenes to the summit rock and view the Capital City by night, while below in a foreground of martial splendour — of the flash and glitter of arms and the swing of the tartan, the pipes and drums of the Scottish Regiments enthrall the audience come from all parts of the world.

Looking north, the Firth of Forth shows faintly in the afterglow of a summer's night and beyond, the coast of Fife is fringed by the myriad lights of the towns and fishing villages ranging to where the Firth opens to the North Sea. To the south, the Pentland Hills, the largest artificial ski-slope in Europe scoring its side.

Nearer hand to the north again, the line of Princes Street and the festival lights of the gardens of that street take the eye eastwards to the floodlit Scott monument, the floodlit Calton hill and nearer, the headquarters of the Bank of Scotland and the twin towers of the Church of Scotland's Assembly Halls.

Due east, now, looking above the Tattoo stands to the Royal Mile bannered for Festival on Castlehill; the spire of the building once the Assembly place of the Church of Scotland, shows as a stark silhoutte against the glow of that Mile stretching down the Old Town ridge from the Castle to the Palace of Holyroodhouse.

St Giles', less flamboyant but no less effective than some of the other floodlit buildings, shows its fretted Crown Imperial steeple topped by the golden weather cock seeming suspended in the darkening sky.

Finally, south-east where the crouching leonine miniature mountain of Arthur's Seat makes a backcloth to the suburbs and to again, floodlight — this time on the dome of the University of Edinburgh above the 'Old Quad'.

As most visitors naturally explore the city by daylight and not necessarily during the Festival (even winter time 'far from the madding crowd' is a good time to tour) let us begin, *not* in conjuring in imagination a prospect from the summit rock at night, but in that same place in the reality of a morning, ready to spend a day finding out what there is to see and savour.

From this vantage point, a reminder that there are five villages within the city boundaries. To the north-west where the

Firth narrows to the River Forth, Cramond village: a place of small yachts, and whitewashed walls set by the mouth of the river Almond, where a ferry waits to take visitors across to Dalmeny Woods and to Dalmeny House, home of the Earl and Countess of Rosebery. Cramond was a Roman Fort — as the inn sign reminds us, and the site is marked out near the old kirk.

From Cramond eastwards along the coast of the Firth to Newhaven village, recently restored, its domestic architecture a reminder of the days of the 'Caller Herrin' — the famous song of that title still sung by the fishwives' choir. A giant anchor decorates the approach to the new housing — an anchor similar to that carried by the *Great Michael*, the largest warship of its time launched at Newhaven in 1511. A model of the ship is seen in the Royal Scottish Museum in Chambers Street and in the United Services Museum in the Castle.

Beyond the shoulder of Arthur's Seat, Duddingston village. The kirk here of Norman foundation, has the 'loupin' on stane' — a short flight of steps at the kirk gate to assist the elderly worshipper remount for the ride home; and the 'jougs', an iron collar attached to offenders against the rules of the kirk in the old days, hangs on the wall alongside.

Duddingston Loch, a bird sanctuary, was admired by the great landscapist Turner when he visited the minister of Duddingston, John Thomson, himself a distinguished amateur painter. Thomson had a studio in the manse grounds which he christened 'Edinburgh'. Thus, when unwelcome visitors called at the manse while the minister was busy at his easel, the maid answering the door could in truth say, with apologies, that the minister was not at home — he was in Edinburgh. The studio, an unusual building seen by the loch, also once served as a meeting place for Duddingston Curling Club, probably the oldest in the world.

The nearest village from our panoramic view, is Dean village, no more than five minutes walk from Princes Street's west end. Once echoing to the muted thunder of the water wheels driving the grinding stones of the mills, it is now a quiet backwater with great variety of domestic architecture. High above the village, the Dean Bridge carries the

Dean Village, with the Baxters' 'peels' which appear on the bridge/inset.

Queensferry road to the west, but the little bridge across the Water of Leith below, marks a much older route to the west. Across this way came the funeral procession of Queen Margaret (after her death in Edinburgh Castle) en route to the Forth and the Queen's Ferry for her burial in Dunfermline Abbey.

'How old is the Castle?' is often asked by visitors. It was Margaret's husband, Malcolm III's father who, when king, won a decisive battle against the Northumbrians and so pushed the English border back to where it ranges now. (One Northumbrian of that era, Edwin, is associated with one version of the origin of the city's name — 'Edwins Burgh'.

However, for visual evidence of that time, the chapel Margaret caused to be built is the oldest building in the Castle and, since the Town spread from under the sheltering shadow of that Castle, the oldest building in Edinburgh. What we see now, of course, is a much restored and rebuilt little place of worship, still used for military weddings.

One more village still to be noted: and kept last, since it is linked with a Castle story. For the first time buildings under Crown Square are on view to the public. These mightily arched chambers, and vaults on two levels with gates and chains of black iron, bring to mind vividly this fortress as it was in medieval times.

These vaults were also used for French prisoners of the Napoleonic wars and Robert Louis Stevenson features one such prisoner St Ives as the hero in his novel of that name. St Ives escaped down the Castle rock and heads for Swanston village at the foot of the Pentland hills, where, in Swanston Cottage, the girl Flora who befriended him on one of her visits to the Castle, lives with her aunt.

Outside the prison walls today one can look down from a gun loop to the sheer drop where the fictional St Ives was lowered on a rope, and beyond the old town to the line of the Pentland hills at Swanston, a village of trim thatched cottages once the holiday haunt of RLS in his youth.

A walk round the Castle now, before going down the Royal Mile.

In the newly opened medieval buildings the cannon Mons Meg — 'The Auld Murderess' is now ponderously enthroned with her attendant ammunition; opposite, a pictorial display in colour photography, prints and explanatory captions — the story of her career and of Scotland's earliest ordnance.

No longer is Mons Meg in drab iron tone as when she was set before Queen Margaret's Chapel, for her barrel is bright with a coating of red lead (in the manner of her days of action) against the ravages of rust. On the wall above, her 'portrait' in minature — a copy of the original inset into the archway entrance by the drawbridge. And three plaques: one records her forging at Mons in 1468; one commemorates her bombardment of Norham Castle on the river Tweed; and the third marks her return to Edinburgh in 1829 from the Tower of London to where she had been taken *in error* some time before.

In 1822 George IV arrived at the Port of Leith (a plaque still shows his landing place on The Shore) and one of the masters of ceremony for the visit, Sir Walter Scott, discussed with the monarch if Mons Meg could be brought back to her rightful home. The king agreed. The return seven years later was a gala day for the folk of Edinburgh, as the cannon, after its arrival in Leith, was hauled in procession by a team of horses with an escort of mounted artillerymen and kilted warriors with broadswords at the ready.

Later, Sir Walter contrived permission to allow the Crown Room in the Castle to be searched for the Regalia — 'The Honours of Scotland' — the Crown, Sceptre and Sword of State. These symbols of the ancient kingdom of the Scots had been forgotten after the Union of 1707 when national pride ebbed low.

In the Crown Room now, see the Regalia in all their glittering spendour. As with Mons Meg, the Regalia have travelled in their time. They were taken to Dunnottar Castle a few miles down the coast from Aberdeen, to escape the attentions of Cromwell then advancing into Scotland, and given into the keeping of the castle governor whose wife was visited regularly by Mrs Granger, wife of the minister of Kinneff kirk seven miles down the coast. Mrs Granger came on horseback attended by her maid and collected cloth which the governor's wife had woven to pass the weary hours of waiting when, in time, Cromwell's troopers and artillery came north and laid siege to Dunnottar having learned that the Regalia were within.

One day Mrs Granger came out from the castle, with her maid carrying the usual bolt of cloth and, helped on her horse by a trooper, set out for Kinneff.

Inside the bolt of cloth was the Sword of State and the Sceptre. Tied round her waist under the voluminous skirted fashion of the time, Mrs Granger carried the Crown. These were buried by the minister of Kinneff under the kirk floor where they stayed for nine years until the Restoration and then returned to Edinburgh Castle.

Such a story of civilian heroism is reflected in deeds by the Services, as commemorated in the United Services museum, the Royal Scots museum and the Home HQ and Display room of the Royal Scots Dragoon Guards (Carabiniers and Greys) all in the Castle — but never to more poignant effect for those who made the supreme sacrifice, than as enshrined in the Scottish National War Memorial forming the north side of Crown Square.

On the way down to the Castle drawbridge, two heraldically surmounted inscribed tablets of special importance: one on the wall below Queen Margaret's Chapel records that Thomas Randolph, Earl of Moray, recovered the Castle after 20 years' occupation by English forces.

This was during the struggle for independence, culminating in the battle of Bannockburn. The year before that battle, Randolph and a small body of his men began a night climb up the Castle rock . . .

The rock at its most precipitous was the way chosen as least likely to be patrolled by the English garrison. This way would have been impossible but for one of Randolph's force having in his young days been stationed in the Castle; he had then, discovered a secret path down the rock which he used on night visits to his lady love. The old soldier was able to guide the band of men up to the walls and, with scaling ladders, over and in — to effectively and savagely rout the enemy.

The other tablet is set high on the curtain wall at right as one comes down through the Argyle Tower archway. From May 1568 until May 1573 Sir William Kirkcaldy of Grange, held the Castle for Mary, Queen of Scots, defying a succession of Regents of Scotland who governed the country after Mary's abdication.

A lost cause for this devotion to Mary, but a stubborn one. Stubborn enough for Regent Morton to ask help from Elizabeth the English queen who sent spies north to report on the Castle's defences and then supplied artillery and men to the Scottish Regent.

On a morning of May 1573, batteries of cannon ringing the Castle from below, began a relentless week-long bombardment by which time the main defence — the King David II Tower — was a battered ruin. The water of the Wellhouse Tower at the foot of the rock having been poisoned by the Regent's men beforehand and the well within the Castle choked by rubble from the broken Tower, Kirkcaldy had no option but to surrender.

If, after crossing the drawbridge, looking back from the esplanade, a sequel to that siege confronts us — the 'Half-Moon Battery' or, in the language of the time of its origin — the 'Great Half-Bastion Round'.

After the destruction of the David Tower when the governing forces had taken over the Castle, the fortress was defenceless. In these times, when intrigue was the norm, when friend could become foe in the time it takes to draw sword from sheath, a castle without defence was not to be borne. Regent Morton set about building that 'Great Bastion', today, one of the Castle's most impressive features, rising on the ruins of the David Tower one of whose gun loops shows even now, on the face of the battery curtain wall below the gun platform.

The Royal Mile begins on the esplanade — indeed a royal way when the Old Town from Castle to Palace marked the passage of king and courtier; when all Edinburgh was confined on that ridge, protected from the north by the waters of a loch (now Princes Street gardens), from the south by marshland

Gladstone's Land in late 18th Century.

9

and the precipice descending then to the level of the Grassmarket.

In early medieval times Edinburgh was separate from the Canongate burgh (canons' 'gait' — gait meaning 'way') for the Canongate community grew round the Abbey of the Holy Rood built by Queen Margaret's son king David I. Only gradually did the buildings spread west up the ridge to join with the Town of Edinburgh, by then building the Town Wall.

Buildings in the Town grew ever higher, unable for safety's sake to expand outwith the Wall until, by the end of the 17th century, the tall 'lands' with us today, had become a unique feature of the Town — and an intriguing state of democratic tolerance developed. Topmost on these lands where the air blew cleaner, lived the aristocracy; lower, the merchants, magistrates and the like; and at ground level, the artisans and labourers.

And below stairs? The pigs, for one kind of livestock. The Duchess of Gordon in the tomboy days of her youth was given to riding a porker up the High Street — then, a noisy narrow thoroughfare of pedlars and booth holders yelling their wares; of lumbering waggons, of clattering horse, and sedan chair carriers bawling for a right of way.

Such a 'land' in the Lawnmarket section of the 'Mile' reminds us of the pigs of that old time, with a full-sized effigy stretching in luxurious indolence by the arcaded front of Gladstone's Land, the house now open to view whose interior boasts painted ceilings redolent of the merchant affluence of the late 17th and early 18th centuries.

Opposite, on the south side of the street, note the Dutch-style gables reflecting the Edinburgh merchant princes association with the Netherlands; and a consequent liking, and inclination to imitate, their more ornate facade. And east of these, Deacon Brodie's Close whose son also a Deacon, is remembered as probably the most two-faced man in Edinburgh's history — a respected citizen by day, a master burglar by night.

The George IV Bridge crossing, separates the Lawnmarket from the High Street. On right, St Giles', the High Kirk of Edinburgh as already mentioned. It has suffered the attentions in Victorian times of misguided restorers of its lower exterior walls — and through the centuries, the firebrand of the military invader and the commercial attention of boothkeepers, their stalls backed against its ancient fabric. The interior, where John Knox thundered his first sermon in 1559 retains much of the earlier edifice: the four

The Grassmarket in its heyday as a fair, with the Castle.

John Knox's House and Moubray House to the left.

great Norman-style pillars supporting the Crown steeple for example — pillars that hold the tattered battle banners of the Scottish regiments of old.

But St Giles' history goes back farther than any regiment's. Three dates demonstrate a span from its origin to modern times. In 1243 the Kirk was formally dedicated. In 1385 the building was largely destroyed by Richard II's army . . . In 1953, Queen Elizabeth attended a service of thanksgiving and dedication in her role as Queen of Scotland, when the Regalia were brought from the Castle and carried in procession to the Kirk preceded by the Duke of Hamilton, Hereditary Keeper of the Palace of Holyroodhouse, bearing the Crown — the first time it had been carried in the Royal presence since the coronation of Charles I at Holyrood Abbey in 1663.

Just east of the Kirk, the Mercat or Market Cross where executions, proclamations, condemnations and accusations were the order

of the day since the 14th century. The Cross, only a few yards from its first site (part of the shaft is original) is still used for proclamations on State occasions.

Opposite, is the City Chambers (formerly the Royal Exchange) completed in 1761, whose rear has the distinction of reaching 12 stories to the sky. Until the end of the 19th century the arches enclosing the forecourt (except for the central arch) had their classical spaces occupied by shops!

In this stretch of the High Street down to the Tron Kirk, a certain difference, a more finished appearance with dressed stone is apparent on the south side. These were the tenements rebuilt after the great fire of 1824 which threatened St Giles' and Parliament House — and burned down the timber steeple of the Tron Kirk. Then, democratic Edinburgh asserted itself again, with Law Lord working alongside labourer, all hands to the pumps in an effort to contain the inferno.

11

Street Lighting. After lighting the way through the darker streets the boy extinguishes his torch in Charlotte Square link horn. (The link horns are still there.)

Across South Bridge to the last section of the High Street where John Knox's House juts out, narrowing the street on its approach to the meeting with the Canongate.

Knox lived for a comparatively short time in the house. It could equally be called James Mossman's House since he, goldsmith in the days of Mary, Queen of Scots, began occupying the place when Knox had newly returned from exile in the Continent and had not yet arrived in Scotland.

The House forms an angle with Moubray House probably the oldest dwelling in the town, built by the Moubray family in the 1470's. It suffers in lack of attention by being in such proximity to its more glamorous neighbour, but is an equally admirable example of early Scots domestic architecture.

If one walks down Trunk's Close at the side of Moubray House, the apse of Trinity College Church is seen at left. The complete church, a 15th century masterpiece, once stood where now the 'Flying Scotsman' leaves Waverley Station. When the railway came in the 1840's the church was taken down stone by stone for re-siting and the choice of its new position was settled only after some 20 years. Although the apse is now all that remains of the original, the altar pieces have survived in fine condition and are on display in the National Gallery of Scotland at the Mound.

Where the High Street meets the Canongate, the site of the Netherbow Port is traced in brass on the causeway. High on the tenement on the north side and below John Knox's House, note a model of the Port in a stone panel.

It was by a forced entry at the Netherbow Port at night, that Cameron of Lochiel and his Highlandmen gained access to the town while Prince Charlie and the rest of his army advanced on Holyrood in a circular move out of range of the Castle guns.

The Canongate, of all sections of the Royal Mile presents the most complete example of a series of restorations modernising the interiors but retaining the facade of earlier centuries: thus, the working family of today have an advantage over the aristocratic occupants of former times. Now, there's baths! Chessel's Court, where Deacon Brodie attempted what was to be his final and fateful burglary, is one of the finest of such transformations.

On to the heart of the Canongate — to the Tolbooth and Huntly House both of the 16th century, both now museums and the Canongate Kirk (built as a replacement for the Abbey Church of Holyrood) attended on

12

White Horse Close, Canongate.

occasion by Royalty as witness the heraldry emblazoned on the front pews.

Near Holyrood, the picturesque White Horse Close whose pleasant courtyard was once a place of much earnest activity for from here the stage coach left for London. The coach houses at the rear show how much higher the road has been built up since when it took a relay of horses 13 days to make the journey south. No coach could get through these arched entrances now.

So, to the Palace of Holyroodhouse.

The young Mendelssohn, on his Scottish tour, found as he walked the ruined aisles of the Chapel Royal a line of music came unbidden to mind — an introductory theme that was destined to become the opening of his *Scotch Symphony* — a phrase that seems to hold in its slow lilting all the pathos of 'old unhappy far-off things and battles long ago'. Holyrood broods in such an atmosphere — a Palace for ever associated with Mary, Queen of Scots.

From such dark mysteries and the confines of the Royal Mile, to Arthur's Seat. To *climb* this miniature mountain, to breath hill air — to literally widen one's horizons . . .

At the summit, a westering sun turns the Forth river to gold. Beyond, the Highland hills rise above the horizon line — Ben Ledi and Ben Lomond prominent. To the left, in the middle distance, the hill of Corstorphine, home of the Zoological Park.

Nearer, the sunlight glints on the glass of the Royal Botanic Garden and on the ordered roofs of the terraces and crescents of the 'New Town' where the friendly ghosts of Edinburgh's literary and artistic 'Golden Age' can be believed to be yet walking the pavements in the twilight of a summer's night.

A return now, to the 'Old Town' where we began our exploration as viewed from Arthur's Seat again . . . but should the summit be too much to venture, the road round Salisbury Crags affords an equally vivid though closer prospect — especially if the walk is taken on the path on the top of the crags to where the rock face splits into a V-shape framing a view that Scott knew. And let Sir Walter who did so much to champion Edinburgh have the last word in these lines from his *Marmion:-*

Where the huge castle holds its state
And all the steep slope down,
Whose ridgy back heaves to the sky
Piled deep and massy, close and high,
Mine own romantic town!

13

INTRODUCTION

La capitale de l'Ecosse est en fait deux villes, la 'vielle' et la 'nouvelle', qui sont séparées par la rue principale de la ville, Princes Street, et ses jardins. La 'vieille ville' a évolué assez irrégulièrement au cours des siècles depuis que les premières tribus primitives des Pictes se sont installées sur le roc du château. Elle serpente vers l'est à partir du château en un enchevêtrement de petites ruelles et rues dominées par des maisons hautes appelées 'lands' mais comprenant également une grande partie des grands attraits de la ville comme le Mille Royal avec la Maison du Parlement, l'hôtel de ville de Cannongate et le palais royal de Holyroodhouse. La 'vieille ville' a subi beaucoup de dommages et maints incendies au Moyen Age au cours des guerres fréquentes entre les Anglais et les Ecossais, jusqu'en 1707, date à laquelle il y a eu un Acte d'Union entre les deux pays avec un seul parlement à Londres. Edimbourg est restée la capitale administrative de l'Ecosse et s'est développée considérablement au 18ème siècle. Une 'nouvelle ville' s'est créée à partir de 1767 et s'est dévelopée dans le style plus conventionnel de l'époque sous la forme d'un groupement régulier de rues, demi-lunes et impasses. Elle a également un certain attrait pour le visiteur dans le style classique des nombreux bâtiments qui constituent l'université et la place Charlotte. Ils comprennent l'ouvrage du grande architecte écossais, Robert Adam, et ont donné à la ville son nom d''Athènes du Nord'.

Edimbourg repose sur sept collines et est l'une des villes du monde les plus magnifiquement situées. Elle a été décrite comme étant un 'lieu de théâtre pur' et l'est d'autant plus à la fin d'août et au début de septembre, époque à laquelle elle est la scène superbe de son festival international renommé dans le monde entier et de son carrousel militaire.

EINLEITUNG

Schottlands Hauptstadt besteht in Wirklichkeit aus zwei Städten, der Altstadt und der Neustadt, die durch Edinburgs Hauptstraße, der Princes Street (Prinzenstraße) und ihren Gärten voneinander getrennt sind. Die Altstadt hat sich im Laufe der Jahrhunderte recht unregelmäßig entwickelt, seit die ersten primitiven Stämme der Pikten sich auf dem Castle Rock (Burgfelsen) ansiedelten. Sie schlängelt sich Mäandrisch von der Burg aus nach Osten in einem Gewirr kleiner Straßen und Höfe, die von hohen Häusern hier 'lands' genannt, beherrscht werden. Hier finden sich auch viele der Hauptattraktionen der Stadt, wie die Royal Mile (Königliche Meile) mit dem Parlamentsgebäude, dem Cannongate Tollbooth (Kanonentor-Mauthaus) und dem königlichen Palast Holyroodhouse. Im Mittelalter kam die Altstadt sehr zu Schaden und wurde einigemal in Brand gesteckt in den häufigen Kriegen zwischen Engländern und Schotten, bis im Jahre 1707 das Gesetz zur Vereinigung der beiden Länder, mit nur einem gemeinsamen Parlament in London, verabschiedet wurde. Edinburg blieb aber die Verwaltungshauptstadt für Schottland und wuchs im 18. Jahrhundert ganz beträchtlich.

Die Neustadt wurde 1767 gegründet. Ihre Entwicklung zeugt von dem förmlicheren Empfinden jener Zeit, das sich in den regelmäßigen Mustern nur gerade oder halbmondförmig verlaufenden Straßen und Höfen widerspiegelt. Auch sonst ist die Stadt mit ihren vielen Gebäuden im klassischen Stil, wie die Universität und der Charlottenplatz, reizvoll für den Besucher. Zum Teil sind diese Gebäude, die der Stadt den Namen 'Athen des Nordens' eintrugen, das Werk des großen schottischen Architekten Robert Adam.

Edinburg steht auf sieben Hügeln und ist eine der großartigst gelegenen Städte der Welt. Man hat die Stadt als 'reines Theater' beschrieben, und das gilt nie mehr als im späten August oder frühen September, wenn die Stadt zur prachtvollen Bühne des weltberühmten internationalen Edinburg-Festivals und der Musikparade wird.

紹　介

スコットランドのこの大都市は、市の主要道路であるプリンセス・ストリートと大庭を境にして別れるオールド・タウンとニュー・タウンの二つで構成されています。そのオールド・タウンは、ピクト人の最初の原始人一族がカースル・ロックに住んでいたところで、以来数世紀にわたり、多少風変りなものではありますが発展してきています。それは、「ランズ」と呼ばれる高い家々の建ち並ぶ細い道や小さなコートの迷路が城から東の方に向って曲りくねり、国会議事堂やキャノンゲートという通行料金支払い場、ホリルードハウスの王室宮殿などといったローヤル・マイルの市でも最も魅力的なものの多くがあります。

このオールド・タウンは、1707年に、ロンドンに唯一つの国会を持つ二ケ国間において連合法が立てられるまで、中世紀の英国人とスコットランド人による度重なる戦いで大きな被害を受け、また幾度も焼き払られたのでした。

エジンバラは、スコットランドの統制の都市として残され、そして18世紀においていちじるしい発展を遂げました。ニュー・タウンの方は、1767年に道路や家々の前を通る道などの当時の決ったパターンをよりきちんと整理して作ったもので、市を訪れる方々は大学やシャーロット・スクエアにある数多くの古いスタイルの建物も目にすることができます。そこにはスコットランド人の偉大な建築家のロバート・アダムの作品があり、そして市には「北のアテネ」という名が付けられています。

エジンバラは7つの丘の上にあり、世界でも最も素晴しい所に位置している市の一つです。それは「真の劇場」として描かれたこともあります。また、世界に名高いインターナショナル・フェスティバルや軍楽演奏のひのき舞台となる季節の8月末から9月上旬は正にその名の意味を充分味わえることと思います。

The Castle of Edinburgh One of Britain's major tourist attractions glows under an evening sky presenting to the onlooker its lesser-known face as viewed from the south — lesser-known but more graphically important than the popular postcard views for this is its face of history . . .

At right, the Half-Moon Battery. Immediately to the left of the Battery, the apartments where Mary, Queen of Scots gave birth to a son destined, as James VI of Scotland and 1 of England, to be the first sovereign ruler of Britain. Centre, where the windows range larger, the Banqueting Hall where Mary once feasted and where to this day Heads of State are entertained. And underneath and left of the Hall, the military prisons, dungeons and vaults, parts of which are now open to the public for the first time.

As one writer of earlier times put it: 'There is no part of Edinburgh's story — from Queen Margaret's day onwards, that cannot trace some connection with the Castle.'

Le château d'Edimbourg vu du sud.

Die Burg Edinburgs, vom Süden gesehen

南側から眺めたエジンバラ城。

View from Above Castlehill   The twin towers of the Church of Scotland Assembly Hall and New College for ministers-to-be are in the foreground. Across the hidden valley, Princes Street, once a line of modest dwellings, first of the 'New Town' and now a shopping promenade with big business in the ascendant.

At right, the Gothic pinnacle of the Scott monument marks the Princes Street of that more leisured age.

Towards the river Forth, the Port of Leith. On these waters, the 'Great Michael', largest warship of its time, was first tested in 1511. Four hundred and eight years later, the folk of Fife across the river, watched where the Firth of Forth opens to meet the North Sea, the German Grand Fleet make formal surrender before being escorted to Scapa Flow in Orkney.

Today, oil tankers nose their long lengths up river and week-enders' yachts bow to the waves.

Vue d'Edimbourg vers le golfe du Forth.

Blick über Edinburg zur Firth of Forth (Forth-Förde)

エジンバラの後に広く広がる
フォース河口に向っての眺め。

The Castle from Princes Street Gardens 'Grossly indecent and disgusting' was the verdict of a famous Edinburgh preacher when the Ross fountain was erected in 1869.

The nude lady triumphantly atop and the mermaids below were too much to bear? Or perhaps the fact that it was designed and founded in France by a Monsieur Durenne was sufficient to condemn it in the eyes of the Church?

The fountain was commissioned for the gardens by Daniel Ross, a city gunsmith; and public money was subscribed to pay for it voyage to Scotland.

What would Mr Ross have thought of its modern coat of 'gold'? No question however that this makes an admirable gilded foil to the dark precipice of the Castle rock. Until recently, this side of the rock was favoured by mountaineering students who entered the Castle in this unorthodox manner to waylay the military for a contribution to their University Charities Week!

Now, the rock is barred to all while it undergoes reinforcement in its old age.

La fontaine Ross (1869) avec le roc du château derrière.

Der Ross Fountain (Brunnen) von 1869 mit dem Burgfelsen im Hintergrund.

カースル・ロックを後にする ロス噴水（1869年）。

Scott and Livingstone   Among the many Edinburgh statues, Sir Walter Scott and explorer and missionary David Livingstone are exceptional in having annual floral tributes to their memory placed on the respective plinths.

The Scott monument, sheltering the statue of Scott beside his favourite hound 'Maida', is adorned with sculptured characters from his works.

The winner of the competition for the monument's design was a young self-taught artist — George Meikle Kemp — who had travelled the Continent studying Gothic architecture, while paying his way be taking odd jobs as a stonemason.

On his road home to his lodging at the end of a working day during the monument's construction in the 1840s, and in the darkness of a winter's evening, he stumbled into the Union Canal in what was then the outskirts of the town, and drowned.

The Livingstone statue is by what was a rarity of the time — a woman sculptor. She was the wife of David Octavius Hill who, although attaining the rank of Royal Scottish Academician, is better remembered as a pioneer of photography. 'Rock House', at left of the flight of steps leading from Waterloo Place to the Calton Hill was once his studio.

Les deux grands héros du 19ème siècle d'Edimbourg: le romancier Sir Walter Scott et l'explorateur de l'Afrique David Livingstone.

Edinburgs zwei große Helden des 19. Jahrhunderts: der Romanschriftsteller Sir Walter Scott und der Afrikaforscher David Livingstone.

エジンバラの19世紀における二人の偉大なるヒーロー、作家のサー・ウォルター・スコットとアフリカ探険家のデイビッド・リビングストン。

Ramsay Garden from Princes Street Between the photographer's chosen vantage point, on this garden's side of the street, and the distant heights of red-roofed Ramsay Garden lies the valley which once formed a giant moat for the Castle's defence. It was known as the 'Nor Loch'. And near this vantage point, one of the battery of cannon which ringed the Castle in the 'Long Siege' of the 1570s fired across these waters — waters which were also convenient in finding out if suspected witches could stand the test of the ducking stool.

When the 'New Town' was built in the latter half of the 18th century, the Loch was drained and private gardens were set out for the enjoyment of the residents of the new Princes Street. (The modest façade of those original dwellings still show above the shops at the corners of Frederick Street for example.) One hundred years later, when the shops had begun the domination of Princes Street, the gardens became public.

Poet Allan Ramsay built the first house in Ramsay Garden in 1750s on Castlehill at the head of the Royal Mile — and we return to that older thoroughfare on the next page.

Les jardins au premier plan ont, autrefois, fait partie du fossé de château.

Die Gärten im Vordergrund bildeten einst einen Teil des Burggrabens.

前景の庭は以前には城の堀の一部でした。

City Signs A collection of these, taken from old-established long-gone shops and places of ancient trade, survive in the museum at Huntly House in the Canongate.

Still evident around the City, and on the way to the Port of Leith, the boot of the saddler, the mortar and pestle of the chemist, the fishmonger's sign; and in the West Bow a sweep's main tool of his trade hangs above the brushmaker's shop.

Newest of all, yet marking the house of a merchant's place of business of the early 17th century in the Lawnmarket, this golden 'gled' with its rodent prey in its talons. A 'gled' — a bird that glides — is an old name for that member of the hawk family, the kite.

When Thomas Gledstane came to the Capital to make his fortune, he bought the tall tenement in the Lawnmarket — the only building now left in Edinburgh with the original arcaded front. It has been splendidly restored in the 17th century style by the National Trust for Scotland. The refurbished interior is a *must* for tourists.

Although now called Gladstone's Land, *Gled*stane's is the more Scots, hence the appropriately chosen subject for the sign to commemorate its best remembered owner.

Un panneau indiquant un lieu de négociations entre marchands au 17éme siécle — un rapace appelé 'gled' ou milan.

Ein Schild, welches das Geschäftslokal eines Kaufmannes aus dem 17. Jahrhundert anzeigt — ein Raubvogel namens Milan (eine Falkenart).

17世紀の商人の仕事場を示す標識で、猛禽類のとび、またはタコを示したものです。

Lady Stair's Close Through this dark entry Robert Burns walked often enough when he lodged in the building with the turnpike stair at right, as one comes into the wide courtyard enfolding Wardrop's Court, James' Court and centre, the former house of the wife of the first Earl of Stair. She died in 1759.

The house was built in the 17th century by Sir William Gray; and following its decline in the early Victorian era, was bought by Lord Rosebery in the 1890's; this time-span is marked by sculptured hands clasped between the dates 1622 and 1897 on the south-facing façade.

In 1907 the House was given to the town, having undergone a restoration in which the architect has exercised his monumental decorative sense to the extent that even one part of the stairway has a corner to negotiate with care!

Inside, a museum collection associated with Burns, Scott and Stevenson — including a cabinet once owned by the last mentioned, made by that fine craftsman and Jekyll and Hyde character, master burglar Deacon William Brodie.

Lay Stair'Close: une ancienne maison où le poète Robert Burns a autrefois vécu. C'est maintenant un musée.

Der Hof der Lady Stair: ein altes Haus, in dem einst der Dichter Robert Burns wohnte, und das jetzt ein Museum ist.

この古い家、レイディー・ステア・クローズは、昔、詩人のロバート・バーンズが住んでいました。今は博物館となっています。

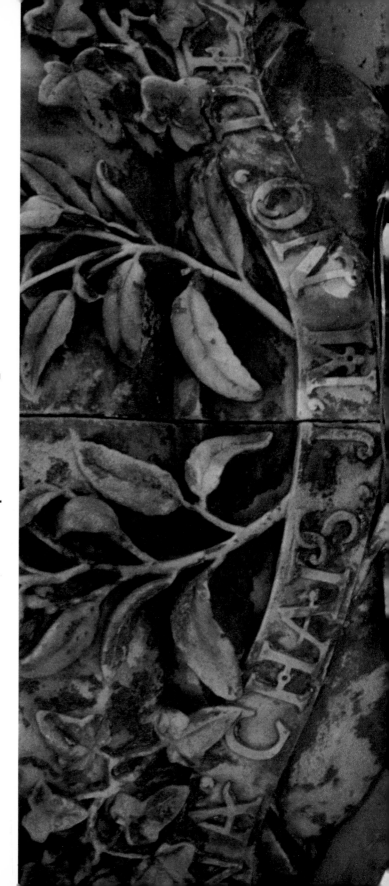

The 'Heave Awa' Land As could be expected, the tall old lands of the High Street, following their deterioration into slums in Victorian times, were at risk through long neglect.

In 1861 a 'land' or tenement in the area of Paisley Close collapsed — and buried 35 people in the rubble.

When the rescuers began moving fallen stonework and beams they heard, from the depths of one mound of debris, a faint cry: 'Heave awa chaps, I'm no' dead yet'. This young unnamed hero has been commemorated by the sculptured head shown here in the entrance to the Close, a few blocks on the north side of the High Street up from John Knox's House.

A better fate met another tall tenement behind Lady Stair's House to the north. The interior was found to be in danger of collapse some years ago, causing the roadway of Bank Street and the Mound to be temporarily closed to traffic. Now, although presenting its original but newly-cleaned face to Princes Street, the interior, with the aid of modern construction methods, has been transformed into luxury executive suites!

Une des maisons hautes appelées 'lands' dans la Grand-rue.

Eines der hohen Häuser in der High Street, die hier 'lands' genannt werden.

ハイ・ストリートにある「ランズ」と呼ばれる家の中でもこれは高いほうの家です。

The Palace of Holyroodhouse

Above the Palace flies the Royal Standard for Scotland — the Lion Rampant, denoting that, in the Sovereign's absence, the office of Hereditary Keeper of the Palace still maintains, held since 1646 by the Dukes of Hamilton.

The twin towers at left are those associated with King James IV who founded the Palace. He extended the forefront, intending to repeat the towers at the southern extent but never realised this scheme.

The Palace as we know it today was the work in the 1670s of Robert, of the Mylne family, master masons for many decades to the Royal House of Scotland.

Thereafter, the Palace welcomed — or suffered, a variety of tenants. James V, father of Mary Queen of Scots was born there. Mary's secretary David Rizzio was murdered. It was a barracks for Cromwell's troopers, Prince Charles Edward Stewart held court there — as did George IV, the first monarch to visit Scotland since Charles II.

In 1911, the Palace came into its own again when it was restored as a Royal House for George V and Queen Mary. And so it has continued to be used whenever the reigning monarch visits Scotland. (George VI, on occasion, is known to have enjoyed slipping out from a side door, away from the formality and cares of State, for a walk in Holyrood Park.)

Le palais de Holyroodhouse où la Reine tient ses réceptions en plein air lorsqu'elle est en Ecosse.

Der Holyroodhouse-Palast, in dem die Königin ihre Gartenfeste abhält, wenn sie sich in Schottland aufhält

女王がスコットランドにおられる時にガーデン・パーティーを催されるホリーロードハウス宮殿。

The Palace Entrance   Here is the centre of the forefront replacing that built by Jame IV. Above the doorway, the 'supporters' of the Scottish Royal Arms — the unicorn, chosen as an heraldic beast special to Scotland, by kings of long ago. The unicorn is mentioned by both the Greeks and the Romans and is also the name of an old Scottish gold coin.

The unicorn is also shown at right on the wall of the approach to the Palace forecourt from the Royal Mile — and there it is emblazoned in its heraldic colour. In Scotland, the unicorn takes pride of place (the dexter side) from the English lion when they support the shield of the Arms of England, Scotland and Northern Ireland.

Much older than the Palace, the Abbey of Holyrood adjoining, now in still impressive ruin, was preceded by a much smaller place of worship built by David I, in gratitude for his life being spared when he was attacked by a giant stag in the hunting country around the Old Town. Unseated from his horse and unarmed, the king when the great beast came in for the kill, grasped the antlers, whereupon he found his hands magically enclosed on a cross between the horns at sight of which the stag reared back and vanished into the surrounding forest.

Thus, the legend of the Holy Rood or Cross.

━━━━━━━━━━━━━━━━

L'entrée de Holyroodhouse avec la bête héraldique de l'Ecosse — une licorne au-dessus.

Der Eingang zum Holyroodhouse, und über ihm das schottische Wappentier — das Einhorn.

スコットランドの動物の紋章であるユニコーンの付けられたホリロードハウス宮殿の入口。

17 Heriot Row *'For we are very lucky with a lamp before the door, and Leerie stops to light it as he lights so many more . . . '*
So runs part of one of Robert Louis Stevenson's *'A Child's Garden of Verses'* — as inscribed on the plate showing in the photograph — a boyhood memory of his stay in Heriot Row when he watched Leerie the lamplighter come along the street.

An illustration of this incident is shown in the 'Lamplighter' tavern at the head of Dublin Street where it joins with York Place at the east end of Queen Street.

The Queen Street gardens facing Heriot Row includes a circular pond with a miniature island in the middle. This was a playground for the young Stevenson; and the story persists that in these formative years of this teller of tales, the idea was born, as he played by the pond, for his classic, *Treasure Island*.

Early in the 1800s Heriot Row was taking shape, as was nearby, Robert Adams' master work, the north face of Charlotte Square where a Georgian house is open, re-creating the 18th century domestic world of Scotland. As with Gladstone's Land, a *must* for the discerning visitor.

Heriot Row — l'écrivain Robert Louis Stevenson a joué ici lorsqu'il était un petit garçon et a ensuite écrit à son sujet.

Heriot Row — der Schriftsteller Robert Louis Stevenson spielte hier als Junge und beschrieb die Straße später in seinen Werken.

ヘリオット・ロウ。作家のロバート・ルイ・スティーブンソンが少年の頃ここで演じ、それを後に本にしています。

FOR WE ARE VERY LUCKY, WITH A LAMP BEFORE THE DOOR,
AND LEERIE STOPS TO LIGHT IT AS HE LIGHTS SO MANY MORE;
AND O! BEFORE YOU HURRY BY WITH LADDER AND WITH LIGHT,
O LEERIE, SEE A LITTLE CHILD AND NOD TO HIM TONIGHT!

R·L·S

Ann Street Walking west on Heriot Row takes one to Charlotte Square and its attendant crescents and terraces but, if an out of the way exploration of this New Town is favoured, go north down Howe Street and North West Circus Place; and cross the bridge of the Water of Leith. First left is Dean Terrace and third right, Ann Street.

Ann was the wife of Sir Henry Raeburn, portrait painter (well represented in the National Gallery of Scotland) and he had some say in the design of this minor masterpiece of architecture.

The rumbustious Professor John Wilson, famed contributor to *Blackwood's Magazine*, and Robert Chambers of the famous Edinburgh publishing house, lived here. Wilson, better known by his pen name, Christopher North (see his statue west of the Scott monument and near the Royal Scottish Academy) entertained the literary giants of the day at No 29.

His daughter wrote that in 1819 her father had set up house — 'in a *rural* and somewhat inconvenient house in Ann Street'.

Ann Street — un petit chef-d'oeuvre d'architecture de la 'nouvelle ville'.

Ann Street — ein kleines Meisterwerk der Neustadtarchitektur.

ニュー・タウン建築の小さな名作といわれるアン・ストリート。

38

Dean Village If one re-traces one's steps from Ann Street to cross the bridge again, then walks upstream by the south bank, the Dean village appears after coming under one of the high arches of the Dean Bridge — the main highway to the north.

But down by the Water of Leith, the village drowses, away from traffic noise. Not that this peaceful atmosphere was always so, for at one time a baker's dozen of mills ground flour here for the townsfolk up above; and evidence of this trade is seen on sculptured stones preserved. On the south east corner of the parapet of the little stone bridge for example, are crossed 'peels' (a baker's wooden shovel) each adorned with three cakes and with the date 1643. At the opposite corner of the bridge, a solid old red-paintiled dwelling rises from the south bank of the river. It was restored by Sir Basil Spence, the architect who studied at Edinburgh College of Art and reached the height of his caréer when he designed the new Coventry Cathedral.

One of the most recently rehabilitated sections of the village is shown here — its Tudor-style range viewed from Well Court, whose solemn brick splendour of an almost Teutonic type of building makes it one of the most impressive groups in the village and an example of a last century philanthropic experiment in community dwelling. One thing the Dean village does not lack is an astonishing variety of domestic architecture in which even one of the older mills have been transformed into modern flats.

Le village de Dean — autrefois un centre de meunerie.

Dean Village (Dorf) — einst das Zentrum der Getreidemühlen.

昔、精粉の中心であったディーン村。

The Royal Botanic Garden King George V's Consort, Queen Mary, noted as the soul of punctuality, was once, to the consternation of officials concerned with the royal visit to Edinburgh, becoming an hour behind her scheduled programme. She had become absorbed with the miniature delights of the great rock garden.

Note the youthful gardeners one sees working about the place: these are the students destined to become head gardeners of some park or, more adventurously, botanist explorers. One such expedition was due recently for the first time for many years to go to China.

Edinburgh's Botanic Garden works with Kew and Gardens abroad in furthering scientific knowledge, for these are all much more than just gardens for the pleasure of the casual visitor.

One of the first 'physic' gardens the forerunner of the present Garden, was situated where the Waverley Station now stands. In 1776 it removed to Leith Walk, and in 1823 to the present site at Inverleith. The Palm House seen in the photograph was built in 1858.

Les jardins botaniques royaux. La Palm House que l'on voit ici a été construite en 1858.

Der Königliche Botanische Garten. Das hier abgebildete Palmenhaus wurde 1858 erbaut.

王室植物園。ここのパーム・ハウスは1858年に建てられました。

The 'Modern' Botanic Garden

Glasshouses of modern design add a futuristic touch to the scene and, as shown here, open air sculpture is set about the sward. A Henry Moore creation dominating the foreground in contrast to the fretted silhouette of the Old Town on the horizon line.

Inverleith House, the centre of the estate before it was purchased for the Garden, now holds an exhibition of modern art — a temporary home for the works which are due to be transferred to the former John Watson's School by the Dean valley.

Exhibitions of modern art abound, but unique to Edinburgh is the Royal Botanic Garden's own Exhibition Hall — an up to date and impressive addition to the Garden's attractions. Here, a cross section of a 4000 years old Redwood; there, a corner of the Cairngorm mountains: and from the exotics favoured by the humming bird, to new plant life being introduced for the production of oil, of fibres — and for food.

Le jardin botanique moderne. La sculpture est d'Henry Moore.

Der Moderne Botanische Garten. Die Skulptur ist von Henry Moore.

近代植物園。この彫刻はヘンリー・モーアの作品です。

44

Edinburgh Floodlit This prospect is from Calton Hill. Foreground right, the memorial to Dugald Stewart, Professor of Philosophy and friend of Robert Burns. The line of light that is Princes Street separates the Old Town from the New. Centre, the giant clock of the North British Hotel and distant left, the Castle. The green glow there, marks the shrine of the Scottish National War Memorial and again, the Half-Moon Battery shows prominently.

Subdued in such a festive scene and in shadow below, the Governor's house — all that remains of the Calton Jail, demolished in the 1930s to give way to St Andrew's House, part of the Scottish 'Whitehall.'

Edimbourg illuminée vue de la colline de Calton.

Blick von Calton Hill (Calton-Hügel) auf das von Scheinwerfern angestrahlte Edinburg.

カールトン・ヒルから投光照明器で写し出したエジンバラ。

The Old Town from Calton Hill
In the more shadowed region at the base of the scene, the North Bridge — the second of its name to span the Old Town and the New.

When that first North Bridge was building, it witnessed the extraordinary sight of a line of sedan chairs in the muddy ground below, (but recently the bed of the now drained Nor' Loch). The chairs were wending their way by torchlight from the Old Town, and containing Edinburgh theatregoers, none more keen, going to the play in Shakespeare Square (the site now occupied by the Post Office) where the enterprising manager of the new Theatre Royal had 'jumped the gun' and opened for customers, even before the first house in Princes Street had been built.

Foreground left, in this daylight view, the needle obelisk raised to the five 'Chartist Martyrs' who were tried in the 1790s 'for tending to excite discord between King and people' (early Trades Unionism?) and sentenced to transportation for life.

Prominent on the ridge, the crown spire of St Giles' the High Kirk of Edinburgh. In its general appearance this skyline ridge has changed little in the last 250 years. Some of these tall dwelling places were natural fire hazards, crowded together as they were. One such, now long gone, was nicknamed 'Babylon' and described as 'an immense heap of combustible material'.

La vieille ville vue de la colline de Calton.

Die Altstadt, von Calton Hill gesehen.

カールトン・ヒルから見下す
オールド・タウン。

The National Monument   One of the memorials on Calton Hill. It was designed by William Playfair to commemorate Scots who fought in the Peninsular war, and intended to become a place of worship built in the style of the Parthenon in Greece. But funds ran out and it was left as we see it today; perhaps more like the Parthenon in this unfinished state than it would have been otherwise, thus enhancing Edinburgh's other name of 'The Athens of the North'.

This line of pillars has also been called 'Edinburgh's Disgrace' — an unfair criticism of the inhabitants of the city of that time, for their contribution was adequate — it was the rest of the Country holding back in giving their financial share which caused it to be left unfinished.

In the intervening years since its beginning in 1822, there have been various schemes put forward for its use — all happily turned down. Although never intended to be so, it has made on occasion an admirable backcloth for an open air ballet company! And floodlights dramatically.

Le Monument National (construit en 1824-9), un Parthénon inachevé.

Das National Monument (Nationaldenkmal), 1824-29 erbaut — eine Art unvollendetes Parthenon.

国立記念物である未完成のパ
ルテノン（建立 1824 年～ 9 年）

50

The Nelson Column One more monumental curio on the Calton Hill — the Nelson column, appropriately telescope shaped. On Trafalgar Day with commendable broadmindedness, the famous signal 'England expects . . .' is flown from the masthead at the time ball. Within the entrance, there is a miniature museum devoted to Admiral Nelson, that signal, and his flagship *Victory*.

The zinc time-ball is raised each week day just before one o'clock to drop back into place on the hour — traditionally, a time check for the mariners of old, training their telescopes on the column, from the Firth of Forth.

In the foreground of the photograph, a cannon with a history — a brass barrel of antique significance forged early in the 17th century in Portugal, when Spain dominated that country as can be seen by the Arms of that Royal House still discernible at the touch hole of the gun.

In the colonial wars of the Far East where it formed part of a battery near present day Rangoon, it was captured by the Burmese; then by the British who in time presented it to Edinburgh for the International Exhibition of 1886. Note on the north-facing side of the barrel a line of curlicue writing by a Burmese scribe recording its capture.

Monument en l'honneur de l'Amiral Nelson sur la colline de Calton.

Denkmal des Admirals Nelson auf dem Calton Hill.

カールトン・ヒルに立つネルソン提督の像。

Arthur's Seat from Calton Hill
The Canongate, probably of all sections of the Royal Mile, the best in conveying the character of old times, stretches in a wide medley of gables and rooftops as foreground to the open spaces of hill and crag beyond.

At extreme right, the pointed tower of the Canongate Tolbooth, now a museum and gallery for exhibitions. Opposite it, the white front of Huntly House, the principal museum to reflect the historic life of the Town. Both buildings date from late 16th century.

At the near side of the street, the kirkyard and parish kirk of the Canongate. It took over in the late 17th century when the Abbey Kirk of Holyrood was deemed unsafe — and the Canongate kirk maintains the Royal connections.

At the apex of the kirk façade, real antlers presented by a previous monarch, from the forests of Balmoral (see page 34) the legend of the Holy Rood).

Arthur's Seat, 822ft high but looking higher with its rocky outcrops and the range of cliff skirting its approaches, is easiest climbed from the far side at Dunsapie Loch. The walk round Salisbury Crags — the Radical Road, was so named after unemployed in 1820 whose mood had been agitated by Radical speakers, were, on Sir Walter Scott's suggestion, soothed by being put to work making this road round the base of the crags.

Le Siège d'Arthur vu de la colline de Calton. La falaise a une altitude de 250m.

Arthur's Seat (ein Hügel mit dem Namen Arturs Sitz, nach dem keltischen Sagenkönig Artur). Die Kliffküste ist hier 250m hoch.

カールトン・ヒルから見たアーサー王の席。この崖の高さは 250メートルです。

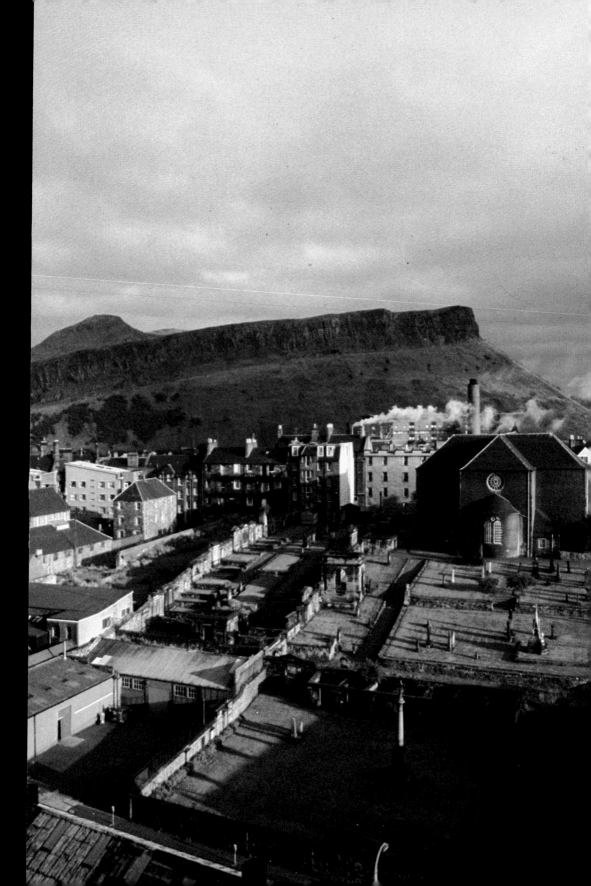

The Bagpipe Maker In the workshop shown in this unique photograph, the Great Highland Bagpipe is being produced by a master craftsman.

The Scot does not claim that the bagpipe is of native origin (Nero is said to have played the bagpipe as well as the fiddle). What the Scot *does* claim is that the instrument referred to is that by which the classical bagpipe music of Scotland was evolved — and that is why we chose to exalt it with capitals to its name — an instrument far removed from the two-droned bagpipe dated 1409, once in the possession of the founder family of the Glens, and now since bequeathed to the National Museum of Antiquities of Scotland in Queen Street.

Thomas Glen founded the firm in 1827 — latterly in the Lawnmarket and no distance from the Army School of Piping in the Castle.

The best instruments have been made from African blackwood, cut up into standard lengths, primary bored, then stored for three years to season. The modern bagpipe has two tenor drones and one bass. Blackwood for the drones, blowpipe and chanter, this latter — the actual instrument fingered by the player — depends much on the skill of the maker for the quality of the music. The only Scottish product, the tartan cloth for covering the bag made from the external skin of the sheep.

Mr Andrew Ross was the last owner of this internationally known bagpipe maker in the Lawnmarket.

Cornemuses en cours de fabrication dans un atelier du marché en plein air.

Dudelsäcke werden in dieser Werkstatt am Lawnmarket hergestellt.

ローンマーケットの作業場で バグパイプを作っているとこ ろです。

Antiques Shops Mr Purves is in St Stephen Street — an opening to the right as one comes downhill to cross the Water of Leith (see page 38 Ann Street). On that downhill way there are others of like fascination. St Stephen Street itself has its personal antique: the arched entrance to the former Stockbridge Market — a relic of the days when queues of coach and horses lined the kerb waiting for the return of their ladies with baskets loaded with fruit and meats and vegetables.

The Royal Mile and George Street have their antiques shops as expected. Lesser known ones grace the fronts of that part of Thistle Street between Hanover Street and Frederick Street.

One other preamble: a window gazers' paradise, beginning at the west end of Grassmarket under the shadow of the Castle rock and moving east along its northern side and on up the West Bow, where half-way it changes its name to Victoria Street. Some of the shops are very old. One in West Bow was a rope shop until recently. It was from there that the Edinburgh mob (see the introduction) took the means to hang Captain Porteous.

Un magasin d'antiquités dans St Stephen Street.

Antiquitätenladen in der St. Stephanstraße.

セント・スティーブン・ストリートの骨董品店。

Metalwork in the City   Private doorways, like this one just east of the head of the Upper Bow, and the imposing gateways to the forecourt of the Palace of Holyroodhouse, contrast well as examples of the art of the metalsmith in Edinburgh.

The Arms of the Canongate — the stag and the Holy Rood, appear in wrought iron on these Holyrood gates and also on the enclosing railings of the Canongate Kirk.

Note, in Hill Street west, the lantern held by an iron hand. Note too, the elaboration of the lanterns flanking the entrance to the Museum of Antiquities. Remember the metal casket in the Shrine of the National War Memorial in the Castle.

Most prevalent and charming of all, perhaps, the lamp standards in the 'New Town' — for instance, in Charlotte Square. The metal 'link' horn at the base of the standard served the following purpose: as gentlefolk set out to pay calls in the evening, they were accompanied by link boys, a link (torch) lighting their way in more shadowed byways of the town until they arrived at the doorway where lamps glowed on each side of the steps; then, the boy would extinguish the torch by thrusting it into the link horn.

Un exemple d'art d'un forgeron.

Ein Muster der Kunst des Metallschmieds.

金属細工の作品例。

The Haggis The photographer has made here, a simple but telling still-life study of the haggis, with its accompanying 'neep' (turnip) and 'tattie' (potato).

The haggis has suffered — still suffers, from the indignity of Customs officials' queries preparatory to its flight to where exiled Scots desire to celebrate St Andrew's Day on 30 November.

It suffers, listening, as it is addressed at dinners celebrating the birthday of Robert Burns, by those chosen to declaim the verses of the poet's *To A Haggis*, and who stumble over such lines as — *Till a' their weel-swalled kytes belyve'*.

And is the haggis animal, vegetable or mineral — or all three—

Time for the plain truth from Chamber's Dictionary: '*Haggis*, a Scottish dish made of the heart, lungs, and liver of a sheep, chopped up with suet, onions, oatmeal; seasoned and boiled in a sheep's stomach bag'.

Sadly, the bag is now often plastic. Sadly, at the time of writing, a turkey farmer is bent on desecration by introducing the turkey haggis!

A final word. Let the haggis remain as its traditional unspoilt self, and worthy of being Scottish — just as Edinburgh is — at its best.

Un 'haggis' — un plat écossais traditionnel composé d'un coeur de mouton et de poumons bouillis dans un estomac.

Das 'Haggis' — ein traditionelles schottisches Gericht aus gehackten Schafsinnereien (Herz und Lunge) und Haferschrot, im Schafsmagen gekocht.

羊の心臓や肺臓などを胃袋に詰めて煮たスコットランドの伝統的な食べ物「ハギス」。